Belinda Kemp

UK SPARKLING WINE GUIDE 2025

JAMIE GOODE

ABOUT THIS GUIDE

Over the last few years I have been tasting a lot of UK[1] sparkling wine, and I've visited quite a few vineyards, too. I thought it would be useful to gather my notes on recently tasted wines together as a guide for those who are interested in exploring this expanding category further. This short book, therefore, focuses firmly on the wines, and not so much

---

[1] Here I have used 'UK' rather than the more familiar term 'English' sparkling wine, even though all but two of the wines in this guide are from England. It's important to acknowledge that there are also some vineyards in Wales, making some smart wines. UK doesn't sound as good, but it's more accurate.

on the stories. There are other excellent books looking at the emergence of the English wine scene, including the following:

- *Vines in a Cold Climate: The People Behind the English Wine Revolution* by Henry Jeffreys (Allen & Unwin, 2024)
- *New British Wine: New Makers, New Flavours, New Ethos* by Abbie Moulton (Hoxton Mini Press, 2023)
- *English Wine: The ultimate guide to discovering English Wine* by Oz Clarke (Pavilion Books, 2022)

But there aren't many guides like this. Of course, these are my personal ratings, and with this comes a strength and a weakness. The strength is that you are getting one person's palate, and with this consistency. If you like the same sorts of wines that I do, then you are in luck. The weakness is that you are getting one person's palate, and with that comes a stylistic preference that you might not agree with. Another weakness is common to all tasting notes and scores, and that is the imprecision of our sensory assessments. Rating wines is not an exact science, and so please bear that in mind as you read my notes and look at my scores. I may have over-praised some wines, and under-praised others – but I hope my significant experience tasting wine makes this less common than it otherwise might be. Many of these wines were tasted at home, given time for contemplation. It's hard to do volume this way, but I find big tastings can often result in wines being lost. There are benefits of both approaches, of course – the peer-group tasting is good for comparative assessment, whereas tasting through smaller groupings gives more time to ask the right questions of the wine.

INTRODUCTION

It's an interesting time for UK sparkling wine. Wine production in the UK had continued to grow, and the latest statistics released by Wine GB show that there are now more than 1000 vineyards in the UK. Lots has happened quite fast, and it has been an amazing experience to witness the birth of a new wine country during my time as a wine journalist.

The birth of a new wine country

I remember back in the early 1990s when I first became interested in wine. I was aware that England had vineyards, but they were considered a curiosity. The English wine industry was a cottage industry led mainly by hobbyists. The problem was the weather. It was just a bit too cold to grow wine grapes successfully on a commercial scale. But such is the appeal of wine that people were trying. I even began growing some vines in my back garden, and also on an allotment that I rented for a while. I didn't know much about viticulture, and the results were decidedly patchy, but I enjoyed it a good deal.

At this stage, most of the vineyards focused on early ripening varieties, such as Huxelrebe, Bacchus, Madeliene Angevine, Reichensteiner and Seyval Blanc (a hybrid with good disease resistance). Uneven and cool weather in late spring meant that although flowering was OK, bunch weights were low, and so yields were sometimes miserly. The vagaries of the weather meant there was inconsistency, too – a factor that continues today, when although average yields are a reasonable 8 tons/hectare, they can vary from say 3 to 12 depending on the season.

My interest developed, and I visited a few vineyards. There was Denbies, the largest at the time, in the shadow of the beautiful Box Hill in Surrey, which is part of the North Downs. Their Surrey Gold wine was at the time a just-about-drinkable off dry white where sugar was needed to counter the searing acidity. I ventured up to Three Choirs, in Newent, Gloucestershire, where they had some OK wines and the vineyard was planted with a training system developed for hybrids in the eastern USA called Geneva Double Curtain. And then down in Devon, I went to a rain-soaked vineyard called Sharpham, who made some nice dry wines, and a chunky red from grapes grown under polytunnels. But it was a far cry from the professional wine industry that has now emerged. We are seeing the birth of a new wine country, and the transformation has been spectacular.

Back in 2012, there were just 1438 hectares of vineyards. As of 2024, there are 4209 hectares under vine, which represents 123% growth over a decade. There are 1030 registered vineyards, a 9.2% year on year increase. And wine sales grew by 10% in this period against a background of falling sales from other countries. Last year was another year of growth. In 2023,

87 new vineyards were registered, and 12 new wineries (bringing the total to 221). The equivalent of 21.6 million bottles were made in 2023, with the 5 year average being 12.4 million bottles. Of course, with all this extra wine, someone must buy it, and this is leading to concern in some circles that we are heading for a glut.

What has caused this revolution? The simplest answer is that climate change (or climate chaos, as it should probably be called) has resulted in a warming trend that means that there's a better chance of getting the grapes ripe. Still, it remains a properly marginal climate, as the difficult 2021 growing season showed, and 2023 also had some challenges. 2024 was full of viticultural hazard, and resulted in the lowest yields per productive hectare since the awfully cold 2012 vintage. But finally the sums seem to be working that mean that larger commercial ventures can realistically hope to have a chance of breaking even. The UK wine scene is no longer the preserve of the hobbyist, and vineyards are no longer follies, although it remains entirely possible that s will lose money rather than make it.

They key development has been the switch to traditional method sparkling wine, and the three main Champagne varieties, Chardonnay, Pinot Noir and Pinot Meunier.

Grape Variety	Hectarage and percentage of planting
Chardonnay	1331 ha, 32%
Pinot Noir	1157 ha, 27%
Pinot Meunier	379 ha, 9%
Bacchus	324 ha, 8%
Seyval Blanc	127 ha, 3%
Solaris	110 ha, 3%
Pinot Noir Précoce	73 ha, 2%
Pinot Gris	69 ha, 2%
Reichensteiner	67 ha, 2%
Rondo	66 ha, 2%

It's probably Nyetimber, one of the UK's most celebrated producers, that we must thank for prompting this switch. They were the first to plant Chardonnay commercially, and their dedication to traditional method sparkling – and successful results – prompted many others to try. Success has followed success, and now there are many top quality producers who are getting it right. One of the keys to this success has been focus. Where existing still wine producers add a sparkling wine or two to their portfolio, the results rarely impress. Traditional method fizz, it seems, is best made by wineries where this is the sole, or major, focus. In comparative tastings of English sparkling wine with competitors from elsewhere, including Champagne, the English wines seem to do pretty well.

76% of wine produced in 2023 will be made into sparkling wine, 23% into still wine, and 1% into other products such as Vermouth. 91% of sparkling wine is being made using the traditional method, 7% using Charmat, 1.8% using carbonation and a small fraction (0.2%) using other methods.

Of course, such explosive growth raises questions about how sustainable this is. So far, there's been strong demand for grapes on the spot market (typically a tonne would sell for £2000), which suggests that the market isn't yet saturated. The big story now is the re-emergence of still wines. Sparkling requires a lot of investment and cashflow, while still wines can be sold within a year of harvest. And right at the centre of this still wine revival are the vineyards in Essex, which is the warmest and driest part of the country. Previously a lot of fuss has been made of the chalk-based vineyards that run through Kent, Sussex and Hampshire – and these are excellent for sparkling wine production. But while Essex has clay-based soils that aren't as highly regarded, areas like the Crouch Valley have such a warm climate that ripening grapes enough to make still wines is achievable even in vintages like 2021.

A CLOSER LOOK AT THE FIGURES

As stated above, the equivalent of 21.6 million bottles were made in 2023, with the five-year average being 12.4 m bottles. Sales of UK wine in 2023 were 8.8 million bottles, a rise of 10% over 2022. Sparkling wine sales contributed 6.2 million bottles to this figure (in 2018 sales of sparkling were 2.2 million bottles) and still wines 2.6 million (from 1.2 million in 2018).

There is clearly a discrepancy between production and sales, but perhaps we need not be too alarmed by this. For traditional method sparkling wine, there is a slow trickle through to market, and many of these bottles made in 2023 will be sleeping for a few years, or being used for reserve wines. This gives sales some time to catch up.

'The large production volume achieved [in 2023] is reassuring,' say WineGB, 'as it will enable our burgeoning wine producers to build up their stocks of reserve wine for use in non-vintage and multi-vintage sparkling wines, and for the small but growing category of NV/MV still wines. Reserve wines facilitate the creation of consistent products year-on-year. Stocks of these wines can take decades to develop, and they allow for greater wine complexity and more blending options for winemakers. As a young industry, building these stocks remains vitally important.'

I'd also add that Champagne is getting expensive. Moët et Chandon's Brut Imperial is now over £40 on the shelf, and fancy non-vintage blends like Bollinger or Roederer are priced in the mid-to-late £50s. The days of £30 Grand Marques are long gone. This gives room to play for the stronger UK sparkling wines, and reports I've heard from retailers suggest that there's good demand for decent English fizz.

Sales by year:

2023: 8.8 m bottles
2022: 8 m bottles
2021: 9.3m bottles
2020: 7.1m bottles
2019: 5.5m bottles

Production by year:

2023: 21.6 m bottles
2022: 12.2 m bottles
2021: 9 m bottles
2020: 8.8 m bottles
2019: 10.5 m bottles
2018: 13.1m bottles
2017: 5.3 m bottles

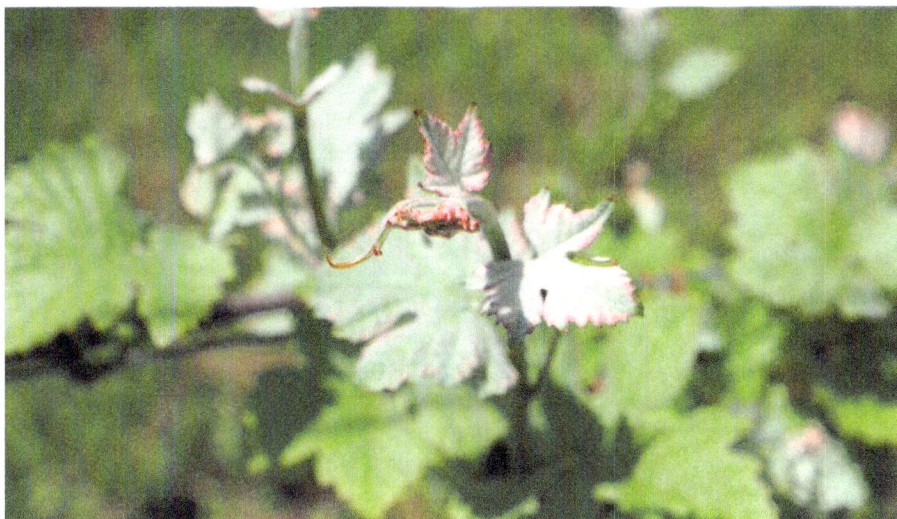

WHY IS SPARKLING WINE THRIVING IN THE UK?

There are two reasons that the UK is now making some very impressive sparkling wines. The first is that climate chaos has also involved a warming trend in terms of average temperatures. This is the most significant change, because it means that it's now possible to ripen the famous grape varieties used in Champagne: Chardonnay, Pinot Noir and Pinot Meunier[2] in most vintages, as long as the vineyard site has been chosen with some care. The second is that the UK has some very interesting soils for growing wine grapes. There's the famous chalky soil found across parts of Hampshire, Kent, Buckinghamshire, Dorset and East and West Sussex. And there are also interesting sedimentary soils called Greensand, which can also give very good results, and in parts of Essex there are interesting clay soils that are now

[2] I use Pinot Meunier because this acknowledges the fact that this variety is a clone of Pinot, not a separate variety. Officially in Champagne this is referred to simply as Meunier, which I disagree with. Technically, Pinot Gris and Blanc are also clones of the Pinot variety, although in practice we treat them as separate varieties.

being used with good effect. Initially, the English climate was so marginal that climate was the key driver of style and quality, but now because of warming trends it will be interesting to see whether soils become more of a discussion point.

The challenges? There's usually plenty of growing season rainfall, and this brings with it disease pressure. Downy mildew is the big threat, and if this strikes early it can hit flower clusters and cause loss of crop. At the other end of the growing season, botrytis can be a big issue. Flowering can be impacted by the weather: unsettled weather is not welcome at this stage, and cool temperatures sometimes mean that the pollen tube doesn't grow well enough to fertilize the ovule, with a resultant loss of yield.

Viticulture for sparkling wine

The vineyard challenge for those who want to make traditional method sparkling is to get ripe flavours in the grapes while still preserving acidity, and not going above 11% potential alcohol. The second fermentation in the bottle adds alcohol and given the conversion ratio of around 16 grammes of sugar to 1% alcohol by the yeasts, and the fact that it takes 4 grammes of sugar to create one atmosphere of carbon dioxide pressure in the bottle, and it's clear that this process will produce more than one percent alcohol for the final wine. In many regions around the world, the threat of too-high sugar ripeness and loss of acidity cause growers to pick before full flavour has developed in the grapes. The benefit of a truly cool climate is that it takes so long to get to the required degree of potential alcohol (and sometimes the target isn't reached, so there is the need for chaptalization), and to lose acidity to a level suitable for winemaking, that flavour development in the grapes has plenty of time to accumulate.

Sparkling winemaking: two philosophies

There are two distinct (but sometimes overlapping) philosophies with regard to making traditional-method sparkling wines. One is currently the accepted, establishment view, and the other is gaining ground among ambitious growers, in particular.

The first is that the base wine is not the source of complexity: rather it is the **ageing on the lees** of the second fermentation that takes place inside the bottle that adds the real interest. This certainly does add interest: the yeasts do their bit, ferment the remaining sugar in the wine (introduced with them at bottling) and then die and break down slowly, adding flavour compounds to the wine. This can take a very long time, and at least three years at normal cellar temperatures, but for real complexity to emerge this way, longer is needed. Big Champagne houses quite like this narrative because they are often working with fairly neutral base wines, which they might make from bought-in grapes harvested at very high yields, or from bought in musts, or bought-in base wines from a cooperative. The extra time on lees also gives a justification for higher prices.

The second is that complexity is gained from working on the quality and characteristics of **base wines**, and then having a relatively short time ageing on lees. This is sometimes a preferred route for growers, who put more emphasis on viticulture, and also the *élevage* of the base wines which might not simply be in stainless steel, but which might include concrete, large-format oak and even terracotta, glass or ceramic vessels. There's also a place for slightly more oxidative ageing of base wines. Of course, the use of reserve wines for non-vintage cuvées also follows this approach. One approach gaining ground is the use of perpetual cuvées for reserve wines, where many vintages are combined.

There are two other ways of adding complexity that need mentioning. The first is the use of various grape-derived concoctions as *liqueur d'expedition*, which can also be a way that dosage is added. The other is time on cork post disgorgement where development is at a faster rate that during triage.

Non-traditional-method sparklers in the UK

Most of the wines reviewed here are traditional method, with a second bubble-forming fermentation in the bottle that the wine is sold in. But there are a few that use other methods, most notably Pet Nats and Charmat-method. The latter style is perhaps limited by the availability of suitable pressure tanks for the second fermentation here in the UK, and also because it's usually seen as a cheaper product. But because of the price of farming grapes, there's a limit to how low prices can be and the wine still being profitable, so this has also hampered the success of this technique. Pet Nats are the cheapest way of making sparkling wines, and they can be fun – and they are often quick to market. But to produce a Pet Nat that doesn't need disgorging takes a lot of skill and quite a bit of luck.

MY FAVOURITE PRODUCERS

This is a personal list of who I think is making the most interesting sparkling wine now in the UK. It's hard to produce a list like this because there are just so many good producers at the moment, but I think it's useful, and the sort of thing I'd want to see in a guide like this. So here goes – my top 15 producers:

1 NYETIMBER

Back in 1986 American couple Stuart and Sandy Moss bought the then 49 hectare Nyetimber estate, exactly 900 years after it was first mentioned in the Domesday book. Based in the Sussex countryside, it boasts a manor house that dates back to Saxon times. The Mosses had the vision to focus on sparkling wine, and with assistance from Kit Lindlar, who supplied their vines, they established the vineyard in 1988. Significantly, they focused on Champagne varieties: Chardonnay, Pinot Noir and Pinot Meunier. This was at a time when no one thought they could succeed in the UK's cold climate, and Nyetimber's original Chardonnay plantings are the oldest Chardonnay vines in the country. The first release was the 1992 Blanc de Blancs, which was made at Lindlar's High Weald winery. The 1993 Classic Cuvée followed. Both wines were brilliantly received, and quickly Nyetimber became famous. From the first vintage until 2007, the wines were made under the guidance of Jean-Manuel Jacquinot, a consulting winemaker from Champagne.

In 2001 the Mosses decided to retire and headed back to the USA, selling Nyetimber to musician and songwriter Andy Hill. The big change, though, was when Nyetimber was sold to Dutch entrepreneur Eric Heerema for £7.4 million in 2006. Heerema was already resident in the UK and had his own small vineyard a few miles up the road from Nyetimber. He decided to invest heavily in his new project and grew the vineyards from 16 hectares up to its current level of 325 hectares, spread over several sites in Sussex, Hampshire and Kent. Another significant step was that in 2007 Eric recruited a Canadian couple, Head Winemaker Cherie Spriggs and Winemaker Brad Greatrix, who have since been turning out some impressive wines. The range now includes single-site Tillington and prestige Cuvée 1086 in white and pink. Currently, Nyetimber are leading the field, and quality from top to bottom is exemplary.

2 SUGRUE SOUTH DOWNS

Dermot Sugrue is one of the most respected sparkling winemakers in the UK. He was winemaker at Nyetimber from 2003–2006, and then moved to work for Wiston Estate. He also began making his own wines under the label Sugrue South Downs (previously Sugrue Pierre). This is now his full time project, and expanded earlier this year with some investment from Robin Hutson, owner of the Pig chain of restaurants with rooms, which has always been a big supporter of English sparkling wine. In May 2023 he purchased the Bee Tree Vineyard in Sussex, which came with a large insulated barn that has now been converted into a winery. He also has a long-term lease on the Mount Harry vineyard planted in 2006 by Tim Renton, advised by Mike Roberts. As of 2023 he gained full control of the Coldharbour vineyard, a 7.5 hectare vineyard on Sussex chalk, planted in 2005. He's been making a wine called Boz from this for a few years. The Sugrue style is distinctive, generally avoiding malolactic fermentation, but the wines are superb.

3 LANGHAM

Langham Wine Estate are based in Dorset, part of the Langham Agricultural Enterprise which covers over 1000 hectares. A while back John Langham decided to test the capabilities of a south-facing slope with a flint-laced shallow clay loam soil over a Cretaceous chalk bedrock by planting some vines. In 2009 his son Justin expanded operations by planting 30 acres (12 hectares) of vines, which means that annual production is now between 50 000 and 60 000 bottles of sparkling wine. Farming is low impact sustainable, with an emphasis on biological control rather than chemical measures.

There have been three winemakers, and it's quite a list. Initially, Liam Idzikowski, now winemaker at Danbury Estate, made the wines. He was succeeded by Daniel Ham (2015-2020), who is now making the wines at Domaine Hugo and also Offbeat Wines, a project he set up with his wife Nicola focusing on natural wine. Current winemaker is Tommy Grimshaw. From 2017 the base wines were made without added yeasts, and with no fining or filtering. They are fermented in a mix of stainless steel and old oak, and there is now a perpetual reserve (a sort of solera system).

The Langham wines are deeply impressive, with a focus of building character and interest in the base wines that is then revealed through the secondary fermentation. They are also very fairly priced.

4 BLACK CHALK

One of the most impressive English sparkling wine operations is Hampshire-based Black Chalk, which was started by winemaker Jacob Leadley in 2015, when he was still working at Hattingley Valley. It has grown and morphed in unexpected ways since, and now makes only estate wines from 30 acres of vineyards (with 35 clone/rootstock variations) on three sites. Jacob is assisted on the winemaking side by Zoë Driver, and together they are producing some deeply impressive wines, including two new prestige cuvées,

Paragon and Inversion. When they bought a cow shed to become their new winery, they were obliged to take on the vineyards, which changed the scale of the operation as well as its nature. But outside investment has allowed Jacob to manage this transition well.

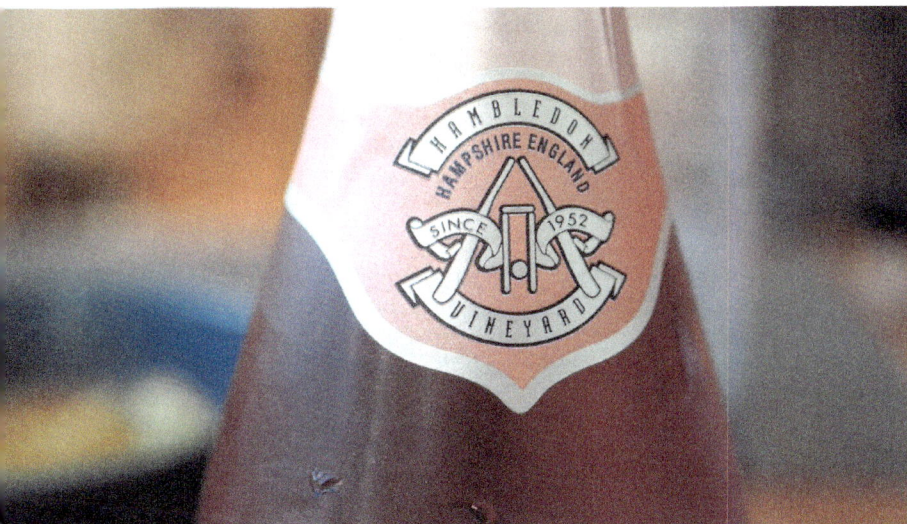

5 HAMBLEDON

Hambledon, a small village on the South Downs in Hampshire, was the birthplace of that most English of games, cricket. It's also the birthplace of the modern English wine industry. In1952, Major General Sir Guy Salisbury-Jones, who'd been a subaltern in the trenches in World War 1, was sitting at home, looking out over his property with his stepson, who suggested he should try his hand at growing grape vines. The sloping field with chalky soils in front of his property, Mill Down House, seemed promising for vines. So Salisbury-Jones took a sack load of the soil to Burgundy, to get it analysed. This went well, and he came back with some vines. He also consulted with his friends at the Champagne house Pol Roger, who gave him some advice. The vineyard was planted and in 1955 he launched the UK's first commercial wine. In the mid-1990s winemaking stopped at Hambledon, just as English wines were beginning to become more mainstream. Then, in 1999 the property was purchased by Ian Kellett, who'd made his money doing equity research on food and drink businesses in the City, and had then trained in viticulture and oenology at Plumpton College in Sussex. Kellett believed in the potential of the site with its favourable climate and chalky soils, and sunk around £10 million into renovating and replanting vineyards and building a state of the art gravity flow cellar, aided by Hervé Jestin, who was for 20 years the cellar master of Champagne Duval Leroy. Back in 2015 Kellett told me that the capital structure in Champagne, where vineyards are owned by growers and the vast majority of Champagne is made by houses that buy grapes in, is a serious weakness for quality. 'It exposes a soft underbelly that can be exploited.'

Kellett began replanting the chalk-soiled Hambledon vineyard in 2004/5, in a test run using 27 clone and rootstock combinations, with the plant material coming from the same supplier as in 1952. He build a gravity flow winery, over a number of levels, with a lift to take the grapes to the top floor where the crush pad is located. The presses Cocquard PAI presses are state of the art, and this is where quite a bit of quality can be gained in the winemaking process. From the start, Hambledon has been based around a non-vintage model. In 2008 and 2009 they sold grapes to Camel Valley and Ridgeview. In 2010 they kept the harvest but used it to start building up reserve wines. In 2014 the substantially increased size of the vineyard (2011 plantings) came on stream. As the volume has gone up, there's a need for creating more reserve wine. New oak is used for 2–3% of the base wines, and Seguin Moreau barrels steamed before toasting are used.

The business plan was for 10 tons/hectare, and for more than half of the years so far this has been achieved. There are now 81 hectares under vine, with a production of 500 000 bottles annually. There are two tiers of wines, with a white and rosé in each, and these are wines that have personality and poise. In 2023 Hambledon was sold jointly to Symington Family Vineyards and Berry Bros & Rudd.

6 ROEBUCK

Since the first Roebuck wines were released in 2019, this has been one of the producers to watch. They have six vineyard sites six parcels of land in Sussex and Kent, all planted to the classic Champagne grape varieties. Roebuck Estates was established in 2013 by two friends, Michael Smith and John Ball, and within a year of the first releases they'd picked up trophies at the two most significant wine competitions: the

International Wine Challenge and Decanter World Wine Awards. The Roebuck wines are consistently good, blending depth of flavour with precision and balance.

7 GUSBOURNE

Back in 2004 Andrew Weeber planted the first vines of Gusbourne in Appeldore in Kent. The first wines were made from the 2006 vintage, and because this is sparkling wine, they were released in 2010 to critical acclaim. Things have moved on since then and now this is one of the significant movers in the English sparkling wine scene, with additional plantings in 2013 and 2015 resulting in 60 hectares of vines at the home site in Kent (clay-based soils, on a south-facing escarpment) and another 30 hectares on chalk/flint/loam soils in Goodwood in Sussex. With winemaker Charlie Holland, Gusbourne made some of the best traditional-method sparklers in the UK. He's since left to work with the new Jackson Family Wines venture in Essex. Further land acquisition means that when fully planted, the vineyard area will total 152 hectares, which is significant. In 2024 majority shareholder Lord Ashcroft opened up discussions about the potential sale of his 67% of Gusbourne's shares.

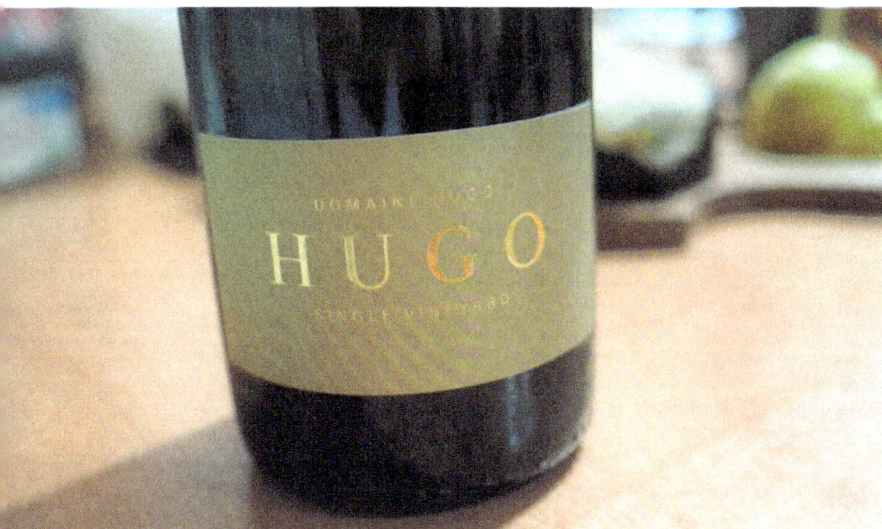

8 DOMAINE HUGO

Hugo Stewart's first wine venture was Les Clos Perdus in the Corbières Hills in the south of France. But in 2016 he planted three hectares of vines at his family's property on the Wiltshire/Hampshire border, called Botley's Farm. From the start he has farmed organically, using cover-cropping, and subsequently he planted another plot with vines. Winemaking is in the hands of Daniel and Nicola Ham, who also use the winery for some contract work and their own brand, Offbeat Wines. The approach in the winery mirrors that in the cellar, and the results are deeply impressive. As well as the traditional method Domaine Hugo, there's also an impressive Col Fondo wine called Botleys.

9 HARROW & HOPE

The chalk-based Chiltern Hills are not famous for vineyards, but Buckinghamshire-based Harrow & Hope are making some of the best wines in the UK. Henry and Kaye Laithwaite (he's the son of famous wine retailer Tony) bought this interesting site in 2010. They have planted 6.5 hectares of vines in a site at the a Thames gravel terrace, which was where the river cut through the chalk hill, and the result is a geologically diverse vineyard. Pinot Noir is planted on clay/flint/gravel, whereas the Chardonnay and Pinot Meunier are planted on chalk with a shallow clay topsoil. Farming is now organic, They have their own winery, and are increasingly using wild ferments for the base wines, as well as oak (around 30% of base wines are barrel fermented).

10 BALFOUR

Richard Balfour-Lynn first found success with his 2004 Hush Heath Estate traditional method rosé (7000 bottles were made after a 500 bottle trial in 2003). But since then, the portfolio and vineyard holdings have increased, and the previously split-brand offering (Hush Heath and Balfour) has been streamlined to just Balfour. The first wine was made by Owen Elias at Chapel Down, and when Balfour-Lynn built his first winery in 2010 he hired Owen as winemaker. Since then, production jumped from 150 tons to 500 tons with the construction of a new winery, and Owen's son Fergus is chief winemaker, assisted by his dad. The range is large and electic, with a strong emphasis on still wines in addition to the sparklings that first bought Hush Heath fame. As well as their 20 hectares of estate vineyards, they also buy from five long-term-contracted growers. Balfour also has one of the best hospitality offerings in the UK.

11 RIDGEVIEW

The late Mike Roberts, who founded Sussex-based sparkling wine producer Ridgeview, was one of the key figures in helping the English sparkling wine category grow. Back in 1995, with his wife Chris, he planted his first vines after he'd sold his computing business in 1994. At the time, few were focusing on the Champagne varieties in the UK, but Mike's vision was for making just sparkling wine from the classic varieties. Initial successes led to growth, and now Ridgeview, whose wines are made by Simon, Mike's son, draw on many vineyard sources and production has grown to 500 000 bottles annually. The wines are classic and consistently good, and this is one of the most important producers in the UK.

12 WESTWELL

Kent-based Westwell are one of the most interesting producers in the UK, making low intervention still wines, but also sparkling. Owner Adrian Pike left the music scene for wine, and studied at Plumpton College. He then went to work for Davenport, a long-time organic pioneer in the UK. In 2016 he bought Westwell Wine Estate, which has interesting terroir: it's clay/loam with large lumps of flint, on a limestone base, and – importantly for the marginal UK climate – it's on a south-facing slope. 13 acres are planted on this site on the North Downs in Kent. First vintage under the new regime was 2017, and with 2018 they've pushed the boat out a bit further. The labels are now very cool, with art from Galia Pike, Adrian's wife. Winemaking is often very experimental, and this is one of the few UK projects to make great still wines and great sparkling wines.

13 EVERFLYHT

Everflyht is an exciting Sussex winery headed up by Luke Spalding, who has been implementing regenerative practices. The vineyard was planted in 2016, and at that stage was 2.8 hectares. The site looks up to the Ditchling Beacon behind, which is chalk from the South Downs. But the soils here at the bottom are Wealden Clay, which is 10-15 m deep. Previously, Luke was working at Ridgeview from 2015-2018 and then moved to Everflyht full time in 2019. The vineyard expanded to 7 hectares with new plantings in 2023. The wines are made at Hambledon, but Everflyht own all the barrels, clay vessels and tanks. They have started using puncheons and clay vessels (500 litres). Luke ferments in oak and clay now, not steel. All the wines have malolactic fermentation. Particularly interesting is their Rosé de Saignée, but all the wines are good.

14 BUSI JACOBSOHN

Based in Eridge, near Tunbridge Wells, Busi Jacobsohn is a relatively new sparkling wine project. Susanna Busi Jacobsohn and Douglas Jacobsohn moved to the UK from Sweden. Douglas was working as a chief executive of Skuld, a Norwegian marine insurance company, and they opened an office in London. They figured that the UK would be a good place to educate their boys. They bought their farm in 2014. In 2015, they decided to plant a vineyard, as Douglas was reaching the end of his time at Skuld and needed a fresh challenge. The vineyard is on a gentle slope facing southwest. They have planted 5 hectares of their 20 hectare property to vineyard, with the classic Champagne varieties: Chardonnay, Pinot Noir and Pinot Meunier, in the proportions 40/40/20. Douglas does all the farming. The soils here are clay-based greensand with some sandstone. They installed drainage tiles to help in wet conditions: it was so wet when they planted in May 2015 that the machinery couldn't get into the field and it had to be done by hand. The 5 hectares produce around 35 tons of grapes, which translates into some 25-30 000 bottles annually. The wines are being made at Ridgeview. The results so far are impressive.

15 RATHFINNY

Back in 2012 Mark and Sarah Driver planted the first 20 hectares of vines at Rathfinny Estate, which is now one of the leading sparkling wine producers in the UK. Four years later, they made their first wines. Rathfinny is located in the South Downs, near Alfriston in Sussex. The vineyard is in a fold in the hills on a south-facing slope. Just three miles from the sea, it is partially protected from the southwesterlies by a ridge in front of them. But it's still quite an exposed site: the proximity to the sea reduces the frost risk to almost zero, but there are strong breezes than caused some problems when they were establishing the vineyard. The average wind speeds looked fine: the problem is most of the wind comes along all at once, in the afternoon.

The plan was to plant trees to act as wind breaks, but the winds prevented the trees establishing properly. So they had to borrow an idea from apple growers and put artificial windbreaks in. These are strips of rubber with gaps in – the gaps are important as they prevent vortices forming. These allowed the trees to grow, and now the trees are 6 m high the artificial windbreaks can be removed. The one benefit of the wind is that the vineyard stays disease free late in the season: in 2019 while many English vineyards struggled with botrytis during a soggy harvest, Rathfinny had nice clean fruit.

The vineyard is right on chalk, and this is the same band that comes through northern France and surfaces at Seven Sisters nearby, forming the South Downs Park. There are 91 hectares under vine, but planted at a relatively low density of 2.1 x 1.2 m (4000 vines per hectare). Yields on the best mature blocks in an average year are 8 tons/hectare. They have planted 14 Pinot Noir clones, and 8 Chardonnay clones (including clone 1067, which a new one, quite terpenic, and which French nurseries wouldn't sell to English producers – they got it via a German nursery who bought it from the French). The first 20 hectares were planted in 2012, and they've added new vines each year, but are now taking a planting break. The house style is looking for purity of fruit and no oak is used to ferment the base wines. Driver is a fan of Pinot Noir and this is the variety that drives the Classic Cuvée. Dosages are relatively low, and this suits the wines well.

THE WINES

This list is ordered in terms of points on the 100-point scale. There's no special science in this scale: the scores are merely a way of ranking and positioning, and I would love to see the spread a lot wider, but then I'd be out of step with the leading critics and the way they use the scale. Few producers would accept me saying that 75 points is actually a reasonable score because I'm trying not to let all good wines fall into a 12-point range like they do now. The average quality of English sparkling wine is reassuringly high. Please note that on some occasions a wine was tasted more than once. In this case, I've included both notes, and there may be a slight difference in score in this case. I've done this for the sake of honesty, and also to re-emphasize that tasting wine, even for a professional, is not an exact science.

Black Chalk Paragon 2020 Hampshire, England
12.5% alcohol. Such refinement here: this is a remarkable wine, with beautiful crystalline citrus fruit at its core but also notes of pastry and fresh-baked bread, as well as pear, white peach and aniseed, with a slight salinity. The acid is beautifully integrated and there's such a flow across the palate. Sophisticated and fine with amazing texture, and almost perfect balance. Complex notes of orange peel, hazelnut and fresh-baked bread in the mix, too. 95/100

Nyetimber Tillington Single Vineyard 2016 Sussex, England
12% alcohol. This is from a single plot, mainly planted to Pinot Noir, on greensand soils in Sussex. This is so refined, nuanced and delicate with beautiful cherry and citrus fruit with a sense of finesse. There's nice concentration, fine acidity and a beautiful focus to the fruit with fabulous length and elegance. Finishes with finely spiced red cherry fruit, and the fine acid line on the finish just keeps going on. Still quite taut and primary, this has a bright future ahead of it. 95/100

Nyetimber 1086 Rosé 2013 England
Salmon pink/orange in colour, this has lovely aromatics of cherry, strawberry and lime, with subtle nuts and rhubarb. The palate is very appealing with fruity lemony notes, some glacé cherry, a hint of marmalade, good acidity and a touch of sweetness on the finish. Complex and layered with some nice savoury intensity. 95/100

Sugrue South Downs Zodo NV England
Zodo is Trouble with Dreams released with zero dosage. This one is based on the 2017 vintage with tiny bits of 2009 and 2011 in the dosage (these were from bottles still on their lees, used to top up the wine at disgorgement). 60% Chardonnay, 40% Pinot Noir. Half large barrels, half stainless steel, no barrels. Tricky frost-affected vintage, so

no trouble with dreams that year, all went to Zodo. Lovely complexity and intensity, with linear citrus fruit and fine spices. Lovely intensity and precision with a tapering lemony finish. Very fine and linear with great precision. A remarkable wine of real precision. 95/100

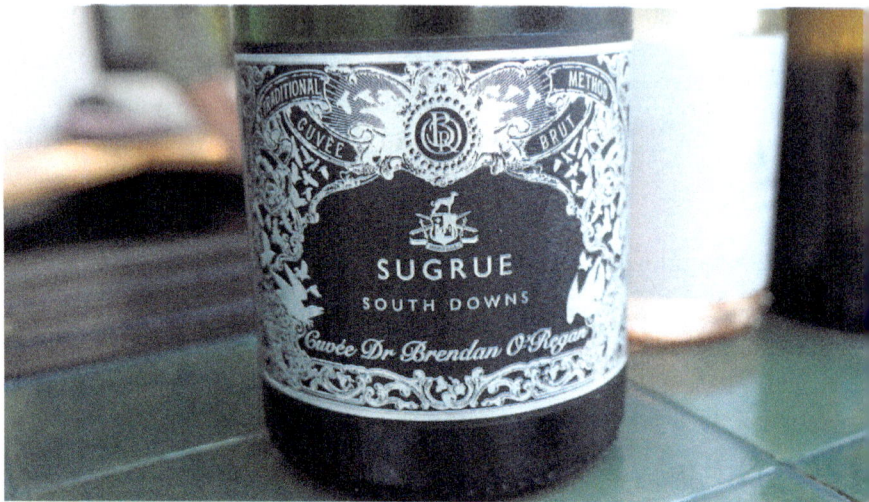

Sugrue South Downs Cuvée Dr Brendan O'Reagan 2016 England (magnum)

Mostly Chardonnay, all in stainless steel. Complex, taut and mineral with lovely spicy framing and some toasty depth. Lovely white peach and pear fruit as some fine spices. Great precision and detail with some chalky depth and lovely acid line. Such precision and purity here with some fine spices on the finish. Amazing intensity here. Profound. 95/100

Sugrue South Downs Cuvée Boz Blanc de Blancs Coldharbour Vineyard 2016 England

12% alcohol. Rs 8 g/l. Lively aromatics here of apple, pear and lemon. The palate is powerful and concentrated, and fruit driven, with pure citrus fruits, a touch of pear and a hint of rhubarb. Very expressive and bold. 95/100

Nyetimber1086 2010 Sussex, England
This is a blend of 45% Chardonnay, 44% Pinot Noir, 11% Pinot Meunier from estate-owned vineyards, with greensand soils. (I think this pre-dates Nyetimber's chalk-soil vineyards.) This particular bottle was bottled on 09.05.2011, riddled on 07.03.2019 and disgorged on 20.01.2020, and the residual sugar is 9.7 g/litre. It has a low pH of 3.01, with a TA of 7.8 g/litre. This information can be accessed on Nyetimber's website, using a code on the back of the bottle. What's it like? The nose shows some apple and brioche, with lemon and pear, as well as hints of cherry and almond. The apple/pear notes coupled with the high acidity, and the significant dosage give a sort of sweet and sour character on the palate. This has intense acidity that's initially quite assertive, but settles down as the other flavours emerge: cherry, lime, toast, honey and some fine spices. It's really concentrated and full, with subtle oxidative hints as well as bright fruit. Such presence, and even a bit of structure on the finish. 94/100

Nyetimber Tillington Single Vineyard 2014 Sussex, England
12% alcohol
78% Pinot Noir and 22% Chardonnay from a site with greensand soils in Sussex. This is beautifully concentrated and precise with aromas of toast, honey, cherry, pear and lime melding together with a sense of harmony. The palate has some innate richness, with peach, pear and bright citrus as well as more of the honey, toast and spice notes, as well as a touch of nougat, and then a long, linear finish. This is so impressive. 94/100

Rathfinny Blanc de Blancs Brut 2018 Sussex, England
12% alcohol. Base wine fermented in stainless steel with full malolactic fermentation. pH 3.12, TA 6.3 g/l, dosage 3 g/l (disgorged February 2022). From the abundant, warm vintage of 2018, this is a very stylish Chardonnay. It has

toast, lime and orange zest on the nose with a slight chalkiness, with fruit to the fore but also some subtle apple and nut characters. The palate is refined with good acidity that integrates well into the citrus fruit core, with some peachy richness right in the background but also some chalky salinity adding poise to the fruit, and very subtle nuts and honey in the background. This is quite serious. 94/100

Domaine Hugo Traditional Method 2019 England
12% alcohol. Pinots Noir, Meunier and Gris plus Chardonnay. This is complex and expressive with lovely toast and spice notes, alongside ripe pear and peach as well as some apple. This has a lovely limey flourish with nice spice and pear fruit. Long, complex and expressive with amazing depth. 94/100

Domaine Hugo Traditional Method 2020 England
Zero dosage. There's lovely depth and intensity here with powerful lime and lemon, and some peach and toast. Real complexity with subtle savoury notes, and also great

harmony. It finishes really spicy and vivid. A complete fizz that doesn't miss the dosage at all. 94/100

Sugrue South Downs The Trouble With Dreams 2014
This is the main Sugrue wine, and it retails at £49: expensive, but worth it! Chardonnay dominant. Half 500 litre barrels, half stainless steel (this had malolactic). Disgorged 2019 with 6 g/l dosage. Complex with apples, pears and spice showing some hints of peach and spice with lovely savoury detail on the finish. Powerful and expressive with subtle toast and nuts. Fine. 94/100

Langham Pinot Meunier 2018 Dorset, England
100% oak fermented base wines, and a dosage of 1.5 g/litre. Lively, fresh and vivid with nice bright citrus fruit and a touch of honey and spice. So vivid, with lovely precision. Complex and intense with a crystalline quality to the citrus fruit. Some delicacy here allied to the intensity. 94/100

Gusbourne Blanc de Blancs 2016 England
12% alcohol. The analysis is pH 3.10 (low), TA 7.9 g/l (normal) and the dosage results in 8.3 g/l residual sugar (normal). It spends 42 months on lees at least (depending on the disgorging run). This is a really impressive wine with taut citrus aromatics and just a hint of bread and toast. The palate has keen acidity nicely offset by some sweetness, and combining the lively citrus fruit with some subtle apricot and mandarin. There's good concentration and a long, juicy finish. I reckon this will benefit from a bit of ageing on cork: it's currently very primary, and although it's impressive, there's some integration of flavour still to come. 94/100

Gusbourne Blanc de Blancs 2018 England
12% alcohol. 100% Chardonnay, rs 11.6 g/l. Nice complexity here: fruit driven and bold with intense citrus fruit and some well integrated toasty characters. Bold but balanced with a good acid line. 94/100

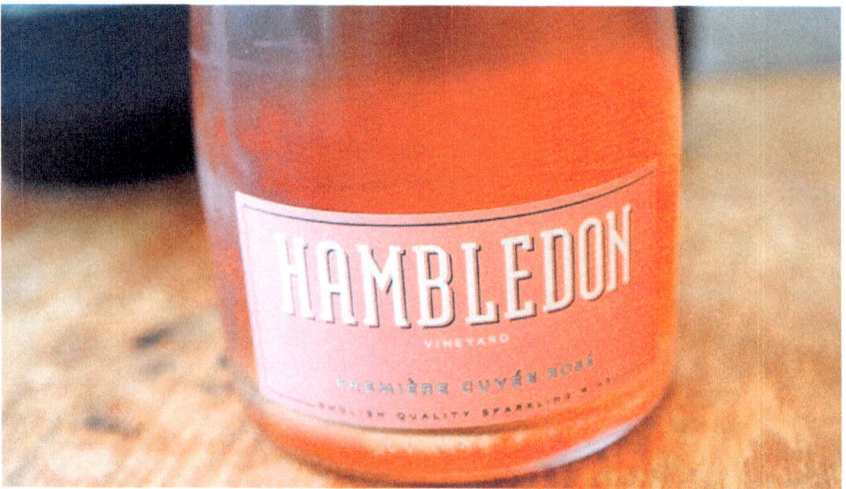

Gusbourne Blanc de Noirs 2018 England
100% Pinot Noir, a wine only made in some years. Very fine with lovely cherry and citris fruit. Poweful but fresh with a bit of grip, and some fine spiciness. This is expansive and rounded with great acidity. Almost peppery! Expansive and fine. 94/100

Everflyht Rosé de Saignée 2019 England
For Luke Spalding a rose de saignee has to have 6 h minimum on skins. 60 PN, 40 PM. This was 6 h on skins. 2 years on cork. 6 g/l dosage. 2000 bottles, and this sells out quickly. Wonderful aromatics of cherry, herbs, a nice green sappy note, with some stewed plum. There's a nice savouriness and some structure with lovely weight and precision, as well as a hint of creaminess. Lovely depth here with balance and complexity, finishing with a hint of negroni and rhubarb. 94/100

Black Chalk Classic 2016 Hampshire, England
This is taut and lemony with some fruity delicacy. There's a bit of melon and pear, too, with some fine citrus and even a touch of mandarin. The core here is a lovely crystalline citrus fruit core, with some of the Meunier red cherry poking through at the end. Very fresh but with generous fruit. Has a nice tapering finish with a touch of sweetness to the fruit. Lovely weight and balance here: this is so fine and is drinking beautifully now. 94/100

Hambledon Première Cuvée NV Hampshire, England
12% alcohol. This is the November 2021 disgorgement of
this wine. Lovely aromatics of wax, nuts, honey and spice
as well as vibrant citrus fruit. The palate is lively and
complex with ripe pear and citrus, a touch of cherry and
cranberry, and also some grapefruit. This is really complex
and mouthfilling with lovely density and intensity, showing
beautiful complexity. 94/100

Roebuck Estates Rare Expressions No 19 2015 England
12% alcohol. This is a prestige cuvée from a single block of
Pinot Noir in Roebuck's Roman Villa vineyard in West
Sussex. It's clone 667 from Morey-Saint-Denis and it
performed so well in 2015 it was bottled and left on its lees
for 84 months. Clay/loam soils. Some barrel fermentation.
It's a full yellow/gold in colour and has powerful, heady
aromas of ripe apples, pear skin and cherry, together with
some almond and honey. The palate is lively and fruity with
nice intensity, and there's a lovely toasty, spicy savouriness
here under the bright lemon, apple and cherry fruit, with
good structure and a long fruit-led finish. So much
happening here: a really distinctive wine with power and
lots of Pinot Noir personality. 94/100 (£95 retail)

Roebuck Rosé de Noirs 2018 Sussex, England
12% alcohol. This is a blend of 78% Pinot Noir and 17%
Pinot Meunier from the Estate's Roebuck, Roman Villa and
Little Brockhurst vineyards in West Sussex. 5% Pinot
Precoce is blended in as a red wine to give colour. Dosage
is 6 g/litre. Pale pink this is superbly refined with lovely
citrus (lemon, mandarin) and cherry flavours . There's a
touch of apple and some slight saltiness. Nice tartness but
it's not at all angular with lovely harmony and just a hint of
toastiness, finishing with raspberry tang. 94/100

Harrow & Hope Blanc de Noirs 2019 England
12% alcohol. 100% Pinot Noir, rs 5.6 g/l. Fine, fresh and
chiselled with lovely fruit: pear, cherry and citrus with nice
acidity. Lovely purity here, showing amazing fruit. 94/100

Hattingley Blanc de Blancs 2015 Hampshire, England
12% alcohol. This is so impressive: it's 100% Chardonnay, 11% of base wine barrel fermented, seven years on lees, disgorged March 2023. Aroma of fine toast, pastry, lime and oyster shells, with real precision and purpose. The palate has lovely acidity beautifully integrated into the complex citrus fruit, white peach and sweet apple flavours, with a touch of chalkiness and some creamy richness, with a bready twist, but the focus remaining on the pristine fruit. Very fine with the potential for further development in bottle. 94/100

Langham Estate Pinot Noir 2019 Dorset, England
12% alcohol. 100% Pinot Noir, zero dosage (rs 1 g/l). So fine and pure with subtle toast. Bright and vivid showing cherry and citrus fruit. Textural with nice complexity, and lovely intensity, showing real personality. 94/100

93

Harrow & Hope Blanc de Blancs 2018 England
12% alcohol. 100% Chardonnay, rs 6.2 g/l. Fine and delicate with lovely crystalline citrus fruit and subtle toast and nut complexity, as well as some richness to the fruit. Very fine, with a touch of almond in the mix. 93/100

Wiston Estate South Downs Blanc de Blancs 2015 England
12% alcohol. From the steepest and chalkiest part of the farm, this was disgorged in December 2020. It's a powerful, concentrated, intense wine with bold flavours of lime and spice, as well as green apple and a hint of pear richness. Some nutty, honeyed notes in the mix, and all through the palate is this core of tingling lemony acidity. Bracing and intense, with its richness reined in by the high acidity. A distinctive but lovely wine. 93/100

Charlie Herring The Bookkeeper Chardonnay Blanc de Blancs 2013 England
Disgorged December 2018 with 4 g/l dosage. Very fine and spicy with citrus, peach and a touch of spice. Mineral but also has ripeness and a touch of honey. Lovely volume here with good precision. Tapered and finely spiced. 93/100

Roebuck Estates Classic Cuvée 2016 England
12% alcohol. Another good performance from this impressive producer. Aromatic with lovely lime and pear fruit, and a touch of peachy richness, with some fine toasty hints. Bright, complete and assertive on the palate with a saline twist to the citrus and pear fruit. Really lovely and expressive with beautiful focus and purity. 93/100

Black Chalk Inversion 2020 Hampshire, England
12.5% alcohol. This is 87% Pinot Noir, 13% Pinot Meunier. Highly aromatic with a slight herby edge to the vivid lemon and cherry fruit on the nose. The palate is bright, juicy and fresh with a tart sour cherry and lime quality, a hint of toast and yellow plum, and vibrant acidity. This is youthful, pristine and finishes slightly sour: a very appealing, quite serious, primary Blanc de Noirs style. Zippy and incisive, and with some potential for development. The acidity is pronounced right now. 93/100

Harrow & Hope Brut Reserve No 8 NV England
This is mainly based on Pinot Noir from 2019. Superb balance with good acidity supporting the ripe crystalline lemon and pear fruit, with a hint of marzipan and fine toasty notes. Some sour cherry and chalk on the finish, which has a salty twist, too. Beautiful. 93/100

Langham Pinot Noir Brut Nature 2019 Dorset, England
12% alcohol. This is 100% Pinot Noir, with the base wine fermented and aged in oak barrels, bottled in July 2020 then disgorged with no dosage in July 2022. The resulting wine has a full yellow colour, and aromas of cherry, apple and hazelnut, as well as a touch of marzipan. The palate has a wonderful savoury character with nuts, dried herbs, hay

and cheese, as well as cherry and citrus fruit. There's concentration and depth here, with some fruit but also a savoury core, keen acidity and lovely depth. With some sweet biscuitty detail on the finish, it's a really distinctive, delicious wine. It doesn't have broad and immediate appeal, but this is actually really good. 93/100

Langham Estate Blanc de Blancs NV Dorset, England
12% alcohol. 61% 2019 and 39% 2018. Rs 2.7 g/l (dosage is 1.5 g/l). Beautiful complexity here, but also a youthful vitality. Incisive, with sweet citrus fruit and a hint of apple, as well as appealing pithy hints and some herbal complexity. 93/100

Langham Corallian Classic Cuvée Extra Brut NV Dorset, England
2018 base with 2017 reserve wines, and a blend of 75% Chardonnay, 15% Pinot Noir and 10% Pinot Meunier. Dosage 1.5 g/litre. Lovely complexity here with taut lemons, some spice and intense flavours, with a hint of marmalade. Keen acidity. Nice complexity here: very fine. 93/100

Gusbourne Rosé 2016 England
60% Pinot Noir, 39% Chardonnay, 1% Pinot Meunier. 5% red wine added plus a portion of saignee. Pale pink. Shows great precision with strawberry and red cherry fruit. Stylish with good concentration and balance, showing lovely purity. Tapering finish. 93/100

Westwell Wicken Foy NV England
Picked between 15th & 24th October 2019 at 17.5 Brix, 12.5 TA. Blended May 2020. 40% Pinot Noir, 35% Pinot Meunier and 25% Chardonnay plus reserve wines from 2014-2018 which make up 20% of the blend. Disgorged March 2022, with a dosage of 8.5g/l. This is really refined. There's a core of bright citrus fruit, but it's joined by some richer toast and honey notes, and fine spices, as well as a twist of cherry. The reserve wines seem to be making their mark here, adding some richness to the citrus core. Very

impressive, with a nice hint of sweetness on the finish. Suggested food match is oysters and monster munch. 93/100

Westwell Pinot Meunier Multi Vintage, England
10.5% alcohol. Traditional method but with no additions at all, zero dosage. This is 2019, 2020, 2021, released 2024. This is bright, lively and complex with subtle savoury spice, toast and nuts, with a touch of honey, as well as lively citrus fruit and a touch of ripe apple. There's a twist of cherry and aniseed, too. Really lovely focus, purity and complexity, finishing dry but not overly tart: the development of the base wines and ageing on lees has added a harmony and finesse to it. There are very few traditional-method sparklers that have no additions at all, and this is deeply impressive. 93/100

Black Chalk Classic 2018 Hampshire, England
12% alcohol. This is a blend of Chardonnay, Pinot Meunier and Pinot Noir, with the base wines raised in oak. Really bright and vivid with good acidity, but really harmonious, showing lemon, green apple and pear fruit with just a hint of marzipan, and tangy grapefruit leading to a long fresh finish. Such a precise, focused wine. 93/100

Black Chalk Classic 2015 Hampshire, England
Debut vintage released in 2018. 100% Hampshire all from within 10 miles of Winchester, made at Hattingley Valley. 45 Chardonnay, 30% Pinot Meunier, 25% Pinot Noir. Dosage 8 g/l. This has a lovely ripe nose with pear and apple and some honeyed richness, but the overall impression is one of freshness. This shows lovely brightness and weight on the palate with taut citrus fruit dominating, a bit of orange peel and a subtle honey note. Lively with some ripe apple and salty lemons on the finish. Dynamic in the mouth: it initially seems to have some development, but then the pure lemony fruit leads the fruit through. 93/100

Everflyht Brut NV Sussex, England
12% alcohol. Highly aromatic with lovely toast and spice on the nose as well as ripe apple and peach. The palate is broad but remains focused with sweet pear and lively lemony notes, as well as appealing toasty depth. This has excellent balance and depth of flavour. 93/100

Everflyht Rosé de Saigné 2020 Sussex, England
20 h on skins. 8 months on cork. 1 g/l dosage. 66% Pinot Noir, 34% Pinot Meunier. This has good colour, with lovely bright but ripe fruit with strawberry and cherry. Nice texture and fruit, showing some notes of negroni and sappy green notes hovering around the lovely fruit. There's generosity but also a bit of tension. Lovely. 93/100

Everflyht Blanc de Noirs 2020 England
80% Pinot Noir, 20% Pinot Meunier, 30% oak fermented. 6 g/l dosage. 2400 bottles, will be released in November. Fresh and focused with taut cherry and lemon fruit with nice concentration and intensity showing tart lemony fruit with nice spiciness, and a bit of grip on the finish. Juicy and expressive with nice richness, showing good acidity. 93/100

Nyetimber Classic Cuvée NV England
12% alcohol. 50% Chardonnay, 34% Pinot Noir, 16% Pinot Meunier. Rs 9.5 g/l. This is very stylish with subtle toast and cream with a hint of appealing cabbage fruit. Good acidity with lovely pure citrus fruit and some green apple. Very expressive with real character and finesse. 93/100

Hundred Hills Blanc de Blancs 2019 Oxford, England
12% alcohol. From the Stonor Valley, this block of Chardonnay is at the top of the estate, and was aged six months in wood (large foudres) before bottling, then it had 30 months on lees. It's a focused, pure, linear Blanc de Blancs with emphasis on citrus fruit, and good acidity that integrates well. Pure and refined with good depth, this shows nice harmony, with a very fine toasty note in the background and some exotic pear and apricot hints on the finish. 93/100

Gusbourne Blanc de Blancs 2013 England (magnum)
Disgorged 6 months ago. Fruity, lively and intense with nice precision and focus. Very fine with notes of greengage, cherries and lemons as well as fine herbs. Sweetly expressive with some focus, as well as some table grape and melon richness. Lovely. 93/100

Exton Park Blanc de Blancs 2014 Hampshire, England
11.5% alcohol. 100% Chardonnay from the first 20 rows of Exton Park's 20-year-old vines: the second sparkling vintage released by Exton Park since the launch of its core Reserve Blend range. 2014 was warm, there was no frost, and there was some warm weather at the end of the season. Six years on lees, disgorged in 2021 with 8 g/l dosage. This is a beautifully concentrated, powerful wine with intense citrus fruit, some fine toasty notes and laser-sharp acidity. Subtle notes of cream and wax here with precision and focus, showing amazing refinement. Still quite primary. 93/100

Sugrue South Downs Cuvée Boz Coldharbour Vineyard Blanc de Blancs 2015
Stainless steel, no malolactic. 6 years on lees. Taut and linear with lovely bright citrus and apple fruit, showing great acidity. Very fine and bright. Appley and bright with a lovely citrus core. Lemony and intense with lovely precision. Juicy and vinous with keen acidity and some fine toasty hints. Savoury detail here. 93/100

Ridgeview Estate Oak Reserve NV England
12% alcohol. This is a blend of 44% 2016, 35% 2017 and 21% 2015. Rs 9 g/l. Complex with almonds, hazelnut and some wood spice notes alongside the bright citrus fruit. Nice complexity here: it's really distinctive with quite a contribution from the oak. But it works. 93/100

Ridgeview Estate Rosé de Noirs 2018 Sussex, England
12% alcohol. 85% Pinot Noir, 15% Pinot Meunier. Rs 9.5 g/l. Lovely bright fruit here: pure with good lemony detail and some toast and spice. Good balance and weight in the mouth with some richness, and notes of cherry and sweet plum too. 93/100

Balfour Winery Balfour Brut Rosé 2018 Kent, England
12% alcohol. 41% Pinot Noir, 30% Pinot Meunier, 30% Chardonnay. Rs 5.6 g/l. Lovely fruit here: bright, pure and linear with a hint of cherry and nice citrus drive. Really expressive and balanced. 93/100

Breaky Bottom Cuvée Reynolds Stone 2010 Sussex, England
12% alcohol. 7 years on lees, rs 5.2 g/l. This is 70% Chardonnay with the balance Pinot Noir and Pinot Meunier in equal parts. Expressive and lively, this is a really impactful wine. Intense with high acidity and pithy limey fruit. Powerful. Not subtle, but quite lovely. 93/100

Greyfriars Vineyard Cuvée Royale 2016 England
12% alcohol. 50% Pinot Noir, 50% Chardonnay, rs 7.5 g/l.

Complex, fine and toasty with nice depth of sweet citrus fruit. Has good intensity and an appealing texture. 93/100

Gusbourne Blanc de Blancs Selhurst Park Vineyard 2018 England
12% alcohol. Rs 3.3 g/l. Taut and complex with rich citrus and pear fruit with some toastiness. Lively and intense with nice complexity. Overtly toasty and biscuitty with real harmony. Needs time. 93/100

Hambledon Vineyard Première Cuvée NV Hampshire, England
67% Chardonnay, 22% Pinot Meunier, 11% Pinot Noir. 2.5 g/l rs. Complex, toasty and lively with some herbs and a nice touch of cooked cabbage. Very expressive. There's good acidity, and it's fruity and intense with a nice linear quality. Bold with high acidity. 93/100

Hambledon Vineyard Première Cuvée Rosé NV Hampshire, England
12% alcohol. Based on 2016 with some reserve from a perpetual reserve and barrels. Saignée method, with 87.5% Pinot Meunier, 10.4% Pinot Meunier and 5.2% Pinot Noir. Rs 5 g/l. Full orange/pink in colour. Nice intensity here with cherries, herbs, cabbage and spice, as well as some creamy hints. Bold limey finish with nice intensity. Distinctive style. 93/100

Hattingley Valley Wines Classic Reserve NV England
12% alcohol. 2018 base with 36% reserve wines from previous vintages. 47% Chardonnay, 32% Pinot Noir, 19% Pinot Meunier, 2% Pinot Precoce (Fruhburgunder). Rs 6.4 g/l. Lovely fruit here, as well as subtle toast, spice, nuts and good acidity. There's a hint of cherry. Nice purity here with good balance. It's quite vinous, and finishes sweet. 93/100

Wiston Estate Library Collection Blanc de Blancs 2010 England
12% alcohol. Rs 8 g/l. Refined toasty nose leads to a lively palate with great acidity and lovely complexity. Notes of peach, toast and lime with some creamy depth. Complex and lively. 93/100

92

Wiston Estate Rosé 2018 England
12% alcohol. 80% Pinot Noir, 20% Pinot Meunier. Rs 7.9 g/l. Deep pink/orange in colour. Powerful and lively with cherry and redcurrant flavours, as well as some grapefruit. Lots of intensity here. 92/100

Hattingley Valley Wines Blanc de Blancs 2015
12% alcohol. Residual sugar 8.5 g/l. Powerful and intense
with lovely citrus fruit as well as some apple and pear, as
well as almonds and a touch of honey. Slight dairy twist on
the finish with high acidity. 92/100

**Simpsons Wine Estate White Cliffs Blanc de Blancs
2018 Kent, England**
12.5% alcohol. 100% Chardonnay. Rs 6 g/l. Fine toasty
aromatics with some sweet citrus. The palate is fruity and
open with pear and white peach fruit, as well as some fine
toast and some creamy detail. Very accessible and delicious.
92/100

Henners Vintage 2016 England
12% alcohol. 70% Chardonnay, 30% Pinot Noir. Hazelnut
and almond edge to the lovely pure, vivid citrus fruit.
There's a hint of green apple, too. Really expressive. 92/100

Hambledon Classic Cuvée NV Hampshire, England
12% alcohol. This comes from southeast-facing chalk
slopes, and is a blend of 56% Chardonnay, 27% Pinot Noir
and 17% Pinot Meunier. It's based on the 2017 harvest with
20% reserve wines (aged in tank) and a dosage of 4.5 g/l
after spending at least 35 months on lees. Lovely complex
nose with ripe apple, honeycomb and crystalline citrus with
some hints of peach and smoked lemon. The palate has
freshness and complexity with some subtle appley oxidative
notes adding a savoury twist, and notes of plum, cherry and
orange peel, finishing with bracing acidity that counters the
inherent richness of this wine. Very impressive. 92/100

**Ridgeview Blanc de Blancs Single Vineyard 2018
Sussex, England**
12% alcohol. From the home vineyard planted in 1995. Nice
structure and poise here with fresh citrus fruit, a touch of
grapefruit and some subtle melon and pear richness. It's
very primary and pure with a zesty edge and great
refinement. Energetic and fine, this is a lovely expression of
English sparkling wine. 92/100

Raimes Family Vineyard Blanc de Blancs 2018 England
12% alcohol. Rs 5 g/l. Lively, bright, pure and taut with nicely complex citrus fruit. Really linear with good acidity and purity. 92/100

Bluestone Saingée Rosé 2020 England
12% alcohol. 60.5% Pinot Noir, 37% Chardonnay, 2.5% Pinot Meunier. 2% reserve wines in the blend. Disgorged April 2024 with 5 g/l dosage. Full pink in colour. This has a lovely direct redcurrant and raspberry fruit quality with nice brightness and good acidity. There's some candied cherry and a tapering finish, with just a hint of sappy greenness. Really good purity and balance here. Bright with nice tartness, but it's not astringent or harsh. 92/100

Nyetimber Classic Cuvée NV England
12% alcohol. Purity is the key here. This is a lovely balanced wine with a citrus core and some creaminess to the texture, with mandarin, apricot and almond notes in the background. Has refinement, a rounded texture and a crisp lemony finish. Quite exciting. 92/100

Harrow & Hope Blanc de Blancs 2017 England
12% alcohol. This is from chalk and flint soils above Marlow in Buckinghamshire, in the Chiltern Hills. It's 100% Chardonnay with 95, 548 and 76 clones, and half the base wine was aged in oak. Aged on lees for 40 months then disgorged in July 2021 with a dosage of 9 g/litre. Farming is organic but not yet certified (this is hoped for 2023). Good concentration here with high acidity supporting layered citrus fruit. Fresh and intense with some grapefruit and fine herbal hints. The barrel ferment isn't obvious, but I suspect it helps knit the taut fruit together. Yet to show any overt toastiness, but there is a bready hint on the finish. This is really good: I love the acid line. 92/100

Harrow & Hope Brut Rosé 2018 England
12% alcohol. A blend of 50% Pinot Noir, 35% Chardonnay and 15% Pinot Meunier from south-facing chalk and flint

slopes near Marlow in Buckinghamshire. 30% barrel fermented base wine, and 7% red wine in the blend. This was disgorged in August 2021 with a dosage of 7.5 g/l. An attractive pink/orange colour, this has lovely aromatics of fine red cherry, some sappiness and a bit of citrus brightness. The palate is vital with keen acidity as you might expect of an English fizz, but the fruit is fully ripe, offering cherries and redcurrants as well as pears and spice, with a limey twist on the juicy finish. Quite a gastronomic wine, with low-ish dosage (considering the acidity) and a lemon and cranberry finish. Lovely tension on the finish. 92/100

Langham Rosé NV Dorset, England
46% Pinot Noir, 36% Chardonnay, 18% Pinot Meunier. 3 g/l dosage. The colour comes from assemblage (adding red wine to the base wine) not saignée. Powerful, fresh and detailed with nice fine spicy notes, and a touch of toastiness. Very gastronomic with spice, cherries and good acidity as well as a touch of mandarin. 92/100

Black Chalk Classic II 2018 Hampshire, England
12% alcohol. There's some appealing richness here with notes of apple, toast and even a touch of honey as well as powerful citrus fruit, with zesty lemon notes and a lovely bright finish. Great balance here, with the richer notes countered nicely by the zippy acidity. Good complexity, too. 92/100

Black Chalk Wild Rosé 2020 Hampshire, England
12.5% alcohol. This is 100% estate grown from the three vineyards (12 hectares in all) that Black Chalk own in Hampshire. This is really lovely with a sweet core of citrus fruit as well as some strawberry and raspberry, also showing some orange peel and negroni hints. There's also a chalky, mineral undercurrent to the fruit. Fine, refined and linear with no rough edges. 92/100

Black Chalk Wild Rosé 2018 Hampshire, England
12% alcohol. This is 61% Pinot Meunier, 25% Pinot Noir, 14% Chardonnay from the warm 2018 vintage. TA 9.2g/l, dosage 6.0 g/l. This comes from vineyards in Hampshire. It's a delicate pink colour, with a brightly aromatic nose of vivid redcurrant and citrus fruit, and just a subtle sappy green hint that adds nicely to the mix. The palate is fresh and quite bracing, with pure cherries, only-just-ripe strawberries and some orange peel and lemon citrus notes. The high acidity is balanced nicely by a touch of sweetness, and the overall impression is one of purity and precision. 92/100

Camel Valley Pinot Noir Rosé Brut 2020 England
12.5% alcohol. 100% Pinot Noir, rs 12 g/l. Nice fruit here: linear and pure with a hint of cherry and some apple, with lovely citrus purity. Fruit driven and expressive. 92/100

Hundred Hills Blanc de Noir 2019 Oxford, England
12% alcohol. This is 100% Pinot Noir grown in the Stonor Valley. Rich and bold with sweet cherry and lemon notes as well as some apple character. This has an innate richness, all backed up by good acidity. Tangy and rich with cherry and spice, and a lovely vibrancy. 92/100

Ridgeview Cavendish NV England
12% alcohol. Beautifully packaged, this is a bright, crisp, pure expression of English sparkling wine with lemon, cherry and pear fruit, subtle toasty notes and keen acidity. Fine, fresh and linear with a juicy focus. Brisk, fine and delicious. 92/100

Roebuck Estates Classic Cuvée 2018 England

12% alcohol. This is pure, delicate and refined. There's a fine toasty note on the nose with some fresh bready character, as well as orange peel and lime. The palate is precise and incisive with a nice acid line, some pure lemony fruit, and just a hint of peach and apricot richness. Beautiful balance here. 92/100

Roebuck Estates Rosé de Noirs 2017 England

12% alcohol. Pinot Noir and Pinot Meunier aged for a minimum of 36 months. Pale pink in colour, this is a sweetly fruited, harmonious, delicate pink fizz with notes of ripe pear, pink grapefruit and sweet cherries, held in line with good acidity – but certainly not too much acidity. There's a faint toastiness here that adds a little savoury depth, and also a hint of rhubarb and sour cherry on the finish. Lovely stuff. 92/100

Roebuck Estates Classic Cuvée 2014 England

12% alcohol. Bright and crystalline with lovely citrus, ripe apple and white peach fruit. Very expressive with lots of bass, mid and treble, with appealing bright citrus fruit, but also some toast and yellow plum character. Really sophisticated and refined with nice freshness and purity, combined with depth. 92/100

Roebuck Estates Blanc de Noirs 2015 Sussex, England
12% alcohol. Made from Pinot Noir grapes grown in the Roman Villa Vineyard foothills of the South Downs in West Sussex. Deep yellow gold in colour, this has an enticing nose of toast, peach and baked apple with some grapefruit peel. The palate is broad but focused at the same time, with apples, pears, cherries and then some patisserie richness. The finish has some keen lemony acidity that keeps everything in its place. Drinking very well now, no need to hold: for those who love a rich Pinot Noir style of fizz. 92/100

Ridgeview Pinot Noir Sparkling Red Reserve NV England
12% alcohol. Vibrant cherry red in colour, this has a core of lovely ripe cherry and raspberry fruit with nice purity. The palate is supple and fresh with a hint of green and good acidity, but there are no rough edges here, just pure drinkability and pleasure. Finishes sappy and bright, and there's also a faint hint of vanilla oak in the mix that adds an extra dimension. An impressive debut release for this wine. 92/100

Rathfinny Rosé Brut 2018 Sussex, England
12% alcohol. 81% Pinot Noir, 13% Chardonnay and 6% Pinot Meunier. Disgorged July 2021. This is an attractive pale salmon pink colour with some coral notes. It has inviting aromas of cherries, spice, a twist of marzipan and some red apple. The palate is textured and smooth, with lovely redcurrant and cherry fruit as well as a bit of apple and some citrus. It's ripe, easy and generous, but has a hint of seriousness, too. Very impressive. 92/100

Hundred Hills Rosé de Saignée 2018 England
12% alcohol. 100% Pinot Noir, clone 115. Rs 6 g/l. A very distinctive oaky pink fizz. Almonds and cherries on the nose. Powerful palate has some woody notes giving a savoury twist. Bright, intense, lively and distinctive. 92/100

Oxney Blanc de Blancs 2019 England
Bright and linear with nice purity and good acidity. The acidity integrates really well. Crystallie with nice chalky mineral undertones and a core of pure lemony fruit. Really appealing: crystalline and delicious. 92/100

Westwell Pelegrim NV England
This is the new release of this non-vintage traditional-method sparkling which has some reserve wines in the blend, and spends three years on lees. It's ripe, aromatic and appealing with some baked apple and toast, as well as cherry and pear fruit on the nose. The palate is powerful but has a rounded character with ripe fruit to the fore: pear, cherry and yellow plum. There's some grapey richness, too. Mellow and rounded and quite lovely. 92/100

Gusbourne Brut Reserve 2018 England
There was a bit of malolactic this year, and the wine is a blend of 64% Pinot Meunier, 35% Chardonnay and 29% Pinot Noir. Lovely fruit here with cherries, citrus and some sweeter notes of pear, peach and apples. Very stylish with nice weight, and a fresh finish. 92/100 (£39)

Exton Park Blanc de Noirs 2014 England
11.5% alcohol. Pinot Noir, 7 years on lees, disgorged in 2022. This is tart and bright with keen lemony acidity high in the mix. There's some green apple and cherry here alongside the lemon and lime fruit, and some rhubarb, with subtle bready, toasty complexity. Flirting with unripeness, with no malolactic exaggerating the shrill acid line. Distinctive stuff, thoroughly English in style, with lots to like. 92/100

Hambledon Classic Cuvée Rosé NV Hampshire, England
12% alcohol. Lovely aromatics here with orange peel, cherry and aniseed as well as some apple and lime. The palate has toast and spice, with lovely savoury complexity and a bit of structure. Toast, fine herbs and some lemons

add real interest here, to this impactful sparkling rosé, which finishes with high acidity and a mineral twist. 92/100

Westwell Blanc de Blancs 2013 Kent, England
12% alcohol. Chardonnay bottled in 2014 and then disgorged in June 2021. This has lovely depth of apple and citrus fruit with fine toasty notes. There's a juicy quality, with good acidity providing freshness, and also wonderful fine toasty complexity from seven years on the lees. It combines ripe peach and baked apple notes, as well a lovely lemon and lime thread that continues through the finish. Such precision as well as richness. 92/100

Digby Fine English Reserve Brut 2013 England
12% alcohol. From Sussex, Hampshire, Kent and Dorset. Partial malolactic, disgorged September 2020, 8 g/l dosage. This is a rich, complex expression of English sparkling wine with good structure and purity. There's a touch of toast, some bread, a lively spiciness and then concentrated citrus fruit with some pear skin and peach richness. It's really vital and there's a lovely balance between the keen acidity, the citrus freshness, and the slightly richer notes filling in the bass end. The dosage adds volume and a touch of sweetness on the finish. Very stylish: accessible and also serious. 92/100

Digby Fine English Vintage Reserve Brut 2013 England
12% alcohol. 65% Chardonnay, 25% Pinot Noir, 10% Pinot Meunier. Rs 8g/l. Powerful and intense with bright citrus and lime, with a hint of honey and nuts. Powerful with good acidity and lovely intensity. 92/100

Digby Fine English Blanc de Blancs Brut 2013 England
12% alcohol. 100% Chardonnay. Rs 6.5 g/l. Intense and lively with powerful citrus fruit showing subtle toastiness and keen acidity. Bright and intense, finishing fruit forward. 92/100

Balfour Blanc de Noirs 2018 Kent, England
Very fresh and lively with lemons and mandarin, but also some pear and peach and a touch of cherry. Very fresh and pure with citrus driving, and then red fruits appearing. This is bright and delicious, with a real tangerine edge. Lovely precision. 92/100

Raimes Blanc de Blancs 2018 Hampshire, England
12% alcohol. 100% Chardonnay from the South Downs, made at Hattingley. 46 months on lees, disgorged in January 2023 with a dosage of 5g/l. This is sweetly aromatic with subtle honey and toast as well as bright pear and peach fruit. The palate is better and a bit more serious, with sweet citrus fruit and very fine toasty notes, showing elegance and some precision, and finishing with bright mandarin and lemon notes. This is appealing and easy to drink, but there's a touch of seriousness, too. 92/100

Squerryes Estate Blanc de Blancs 2015 England
12% alcohol. Rs 7.5 g/l. Lively and bright with good acidity and subtle creaminess. Nice fruit presence here: crystalline and quite long with some toasty notes. 92/100

Weyborne Family Estate Reserve 2018 West Sussex, England
12% alcohol. 61% Chardonnay, 34% Pinot Noir and 5% Pinot Meunier with fruit coming from the oldest plot on this, 1 acre in the Diddy Field, planted in 2004. At 160m, it's the highest point of the estate, making it quite marginal in the UK climate, although it is south facing. 3% fermented in barrel, the rest in stainless steel. This was disgorged in 2021 with zero dosage. Made in a slightly oxidative style this has a lovely nose of ripe apple, pear and lemon with subtle toasty notes. On the palate it shows well integrated acidity and notes of almond and brioche as well as herb-tinted lemon and pear fruit. Nice complexity here: well balanced and delicious, if a little ambitiously priced. 92/100

Domaine Hugo Botleys Col Fondo 2022 England
Cloudy, spicy and yeasty, this is bright with lovely acidity and energy, with notes of subtle toast, meal and citrus, with some orange peel. 92/100

Denbies Estate Cubitt Blanc de Blancs 2016 England
12% alcohol. 100% Chardonnay. Rs 8 g/l. Cream and toast notes as well as citrus and pear with nice depth to the sweet citrus fruit. There are also some waxy hints with some almond and pear complexity. 92/100

The Grange Hampshire Classic NV England
12% alcohol. This has 21% reserve wine in the blend and is a blend of the three classic varieties, rs 9 g/l. Fruity and bright with some fine toasty notes. Good precision here with bright citrus, pear and white peach fruit. 92/100

Whinyard Rocks Col Rondo 2021 Wales
10.3% alcohol. This is made from Rondo, a hybrid with good resistance to downy mildew created in 1964 by Helmut Becker, with some Asian Vitis in the mix, crossed with Sankt Laurent as the vinifera partner. This was fermented and then bottled with some sugar to create the bubbles in a Col Fondo style, and with no additions (including sulfites) and no disgorgement. It's joyously richly coloured and has aromas of crushed raspberries and black cherries, with some green hints. In the mouth this is tart and dry with beautiful pure, fresh berry fruits, with a nice spicy, tangy bite. Some hints of liqourice, too, with a lovely focused, tart quality to the fruit. Brilliantly done. 92/100

Flint Vineyards Venn Multi Vintage NV England
12.5% alcohol. This is a blend of 2016/2017/2018 vintages, bottled in 2019 and then disgorged in 2022 with a dosage of 5 g/litre. Half of the bottles will be kept back and disgorged in two years' time. Very fine, fruity and delicate with nice precision to the citrus and pear fruit, with some crisp green apple. There's a fine spiciness, but the emphasis is on the pure fruit, with some subtle saline hints and a tapering finish, as well as some delicate green hints. This is really appealing with nice depth and focus, and really nice balance between the acidity and dosage. Very stylish. 91/100

Simpsons Wine Estate Chalklands Vintage Reserve 2019 Kent, England
12.5% alcohol. 40% Pinot Noir, 30% Chardonnay, 30% Pinot Meunier. Rs 2.1 g/l. Lively and bright with a herby edge to the sweet pear and cherry fruit, with some nice citrus. Pure and quite linear. 91/100

Henners Brut Rosé NV England
12% alcohol. This says non vintage but it's 100% 2018. 65% Pinot Meunier, 35% Pinot Noir, rs 6 g/l. Sappy green edge to the nose as well as some pure citrus fruit with a touch of cherry. Lovely balance here. 91/100

Candover Brook Brut Rosé NV England
12% alcohol. 55% Chardonnay, 33% Pinot Noir, 12% Pinot Meunier. Rs 9 g/litre. Subtle toast with nice purity to the cherry and lemon fruit, with some pear, too. Fruit driven and nicely textured. 91/100

Greyfriars Vineyard Blanc de Blancs 2015 England
12% alcohol. 100% Chardonnay. Overtly toasty and lively with a nice intensity. Shows powerful citrus fruit and some creamy hints, with high acidity. 91/100

Balfour Brut Rosé 2017 Kent, England
12% alcohol. Three classic Champagne grapes, from the top plots at Hush Heath Estate. Pale salmon pink in colour, this is a vibrantly fruity rosé with some redcurrant and blackberry notes, as well as a sweet citrus core. Lovely fruit, keen acidity balanced well by some dosage, and a bright finish. Impressive wine, with pure fruit to the fore. 91/100

Langham Corallian Classic Cuvée Extra Brut NV Dorset, England
12% alcohol. 62% Chardonnay, 29% Pinot Noir, 9% Pinot Meunier. 90% from 2017, 10% reserve wines. Disgorged December 2020, 2 g/litre dosage. Rich but also saline and fresh with some walnut and spice savouriness, and a slight cheesiness that's not unpleasant. This is bright and layered, but also nicely rich with some baked apple and pear notes. Lots of flavour here, but with some finesse, with lovely acidity under everything else. 91/100

Ridgeview Fitzrovia Rosé NV England
12% alcohol.This is delightful. A full pink in colour, it's fresh with a subtle honied edge to the crisp, textured cherry and strawberry fruit. Lovely brisk fruit here, with nice acidity, but not too much. Stylish and appealing, in a gastronomic mould. 91/100

Westwell Blanc de Blancs Zero Dosage 2013 England
12% alcohol. Disgorged in November 2023. This wine was bottled by the previous owners, but Adrian and Galia have left it sleeping on its lees for 9 years. 500 bottles of this have just been released. It's lively and chiselled with taut citrus fruit showing high acidity and a dry finish. Tending slightly to austerity but with such precision and a lovely mineral quality from such a long time on lees. Nice purity and refinement, and with a long lemony finish. Classic English in style, and doesn't need any dosage which would be like turning the bass up too high: it's a wine that wants to be tight and focused. 91/100

Leonardslee Blanc de Blancs 2020 Sussex, England
12.7% alcohol. The base wine was fermented in a mix of 25% oak barrels and 75% stainless steel. This was disgorged in April 2026 with a dosage of 6 g/l, and the pH is 2.99, with a TA of 8.5 g/litre. This is rich with bold, spice-laden citrus fruit, showing some notes of toast and aniseed, as well as a slight saltiness. It's a rich, impactful Blanc de Blancs with peach and pear as well as lively citrus, finishing with some pithiness and structure. Impressive in this richer style, with the potential for some further development in bottle. 91/100

Vagabond Pét Not Brut Nature 2022 England
12% alcohol. Pinot Noir and Pinot Precoce from Hidden Spring Vineyard in Sussex and Yew Tree Vineyard in Oxfordshire. This is joyful, with pure watermelon and cherry fruit as well as some apple and pear, and then some subtle reductive hints. Slightly cloudy with a spicy bite, this is so fresh and detailed, and finishes dry. Non-disgorged, and all the better for it. Has some smoky, spicy minerality in the background. Lovely stuff. 91/100

Vagabond Pét Not Brut Nature 2022 England
Col Fondo style. Nice bright citrus with some cherry and redcurrant notes. This is cloudy with nice texture and freshness. I like the energy and brightness. 91/100

Chapel Down Grand Reserve 2018 England
12% alcohol. 60% Chardonnay, 28% Pinot Noir, 12% Pinot Meunier. 7 g/l rs. Bright and expressive with nice fruit: pear, citrus and white peach. Very subtle toast. Nicely focused. 91/100

Whinyard Rocks Pet Nat 2021 Wales
10% alcohol. This is a blend of 70% Solaris and 30% Ortega, with some skin maceration and then co-fermentation in stainless steel. Bottled with just a bit of sugar left, then disgorged by hand. No added sulfites. A full golden orange colour this is wonderfully aromatic with exotic peach notes. In the mouth it is bright with fresh citrus (mandarin and

lime) as well as more peach and pear characters. Vivid and intense, with keen acidity making its presence felt but not getting in the way. Lovely pure fruit flavours here. 91/100

Hundred Hills Blanc de Noirs 2019 England
12% alcohol. 100% Pinot Noir, clone 870. Rs 5 g/l. Fruity and lively with nice pear and cherry notes as well as some bright lemons. Nice fruit focus here with presence and brightness. 91/100

Wyfold Vineyard Rosé 2018 England
12% alcohol. 40% Chardonnay, 40% Pinot Noir, 20% Pinot Meunier. Rs 7.4 g/l. Fresh, pure and bright with a nice open toasty edge to the pleasant citrus fruit. This has a sense of harmony and purity with a touch of creaminess and some richness. 91/100

90

Chapel Down Rosé NV England
12% alcohol. This is 62% Chardonnay, 24% Pinot Noir, 9% Pinot Meunier, 3% Pinot Blanc, 2% Pinot Precoce. 27% reserve wines, rs 8 g/l. Very pale pink in colour, this is juicy, linear and focused with some cherry, pear and lime fruit. Pure with good acidity. 90/100

Denbies Estate Greenfields NV England
12% alcohol. 56% Pinot Noir, 32% Chardonnay, 12% Pinot Meunier. Rs 10 g/l. Pure and fruity with nice pear and citrus fruit with a touch of spice. Nice acidity here: this is linear and focused with nice fruit. 90/100

Exton Park Reserve Blend RB28 Blanc de Noirs NV Hampshire, England
11.5% alcohol. 100% Pinot Noir, from 28 reserve wines blended together across vintages, with the oldest from 2011. Dosage is 10 g/litre. This is tight, focused and quite intense with some cherry and citrus fruit, as well as some

savoury straw, herb and vomit (in the nicest possible way) characters. There's high acidity, and a structured edge to this wine, suggesting that it might well develop nicely in bottle. At the moment it's very primary, and while it's complex and layered, it's a bit aggressive. Finishes tart and lemony. 90/100

Plumpton Centre of Excellence Brut Classic NV England
12% alcohol. 45% Chardonnay, 41% Pinot Noir, 14% Pinot Meunier. Bottled August 2020, disgorged July 2022. A rich style of sparkling wine with some oxidative hints and notes of ripe apple, marmalade and just a touch of peach and toast. The palate shows cherry and citrus brightness under all this rich patina, and it shows good depth of fruit. I like the balance and this is well made in that rich slightly oxidative style. 90/100

Candover Brook Brut NV England
12% alcohol. 58% Chardonnay, 28% Pinot Noir, 14% Pinot Meunier. Rs 5.75 g/l. Nice acid line. This is pure and focused with nice linear citrus fruit and a good acid line. 90/100

Wyfold Vineyard Brut 2016 England
12% alcohol. Wyfold is Barbara Laithwaite's 2 hectare south Oxfordshire Estate, planted on gravel-over-chalk soils at 120 m, which is high for the UK: this is a cool sitre. This is a Chardonnay-led blend made by her son Henry at Harrow & Hope. There's some rich toast and honey character on the nose, with sweet apple and pear fruit as well as some lemon. The palate is bright, with good acidity, and plenty of flavour: tart cherry, lemon and some vivid sherbet notes on the finish. Finishes with keen acidity. 90/100

Ridgeview Bloomsbury NV England

12% alcohol. 2024 release. This is the main wine of respected English sparkling wine producer Ridgeview, made from grapes sourced from around the south of England, and spending around 18 months on lees. As you'd expect from this lees ageing, this is a fruit forward wine with a lovely direct lemony focus, but also some white peach and pear notes, as well as a hint of honey and fresh-baked bread. It has good acidity (the pH is 3.03) but this integrates nicely, and the dosage of 6.5 g/l is really well judged. Classy stuff. 90/100

Hencote Evolution 2021 Shropshire, England

11% alcohol. This blend of 75% Seyval Blanc and 25% Pinot Meunier only spends a short time on lees: it's all about the fruit. Bottled with quite a high dosage of 11.3 g/litre. Richly flavoured with ripe apple, pear and even some peach fruit with some sweetness, as well as good acidity. Notes of toast and spice, too. Lots of flavour here, with good concentration and nice balance between the sweetness and the acidity. 90/100

Wyfold Vineyard Brut Rosé 2017 England

12% alcohol. Grapes grown by Barbara Laithwaite in Oxfordshire transformed into fizz by son Henry at Harrow and Hope in Buckinghamshire. Attractive pink/orange colour. Lively and fruity and intense with nice citrus drive

– some mandarin, lime and grapefruit characters. Good intensity and a tart finish. Dry and vibrant. 90/100

Wyfold Vineyard Brut 2017 England
12% alcohol. 50% Chardonnay, 40% Pinot Noir, 10% Pinot Meunier. 8.5 g/l rs. Lovely fruit here: rounded sweet cherries and pear and a hint of sweetness. Lovely fruit expression. Rounded. 90/100

Wyfold Vineyard Brut Rosé 2018 England
12% alcohol. Aromatic nose of bright berry fruit with strawberry and raspberry and cranberry notes. The palate is bright with lovely red fruit quality and nice acidity. Some creamy hints on the mid palate with a touch of custard. Fruit forward and appealing, this is the taste of early summer. 90/100

Leonardslee Brut Reserve 2021 Sussex, England
11.9% alcohol. 70% Chardonnay, 20% Pinot Noir, 10% Pinot Meunier. Base wines are 20% fermented in oak, and 6% reserve wine is added. 30 months on lees, disgorged in May 2024 with a dosage of 7.5 g/l, pH 3.08, TA 8.9 g/l. This is quite rich with some toast and cherry notes as well as pear, white peach and citrus. Nice acid line integrates well with the bold fruit. This is a rich style, but has nice balancing acidity. Very stylish and impactful, finishing with some sour cherry. 90/100

Leonardslee Brut Rosé 2021 Sussex, England
11.85% alcohol. 56% Chardonnay, 31% Pinot Noir, 3% Pinot Meunier, 10% Pinotage. Stainless steel ferment. Dosage 9 g/l, pH 3.06, TA 9.1 g/l. Pale pink in colour, this has bold, bright flavours of cherry, pear and citrus. It's fruit-driven with keen acidity as well as a touch of sweetness. Bright, lively and energetic with nice intensity to the fruit. Finishes nicely tart. 90/100

Bride Valley Blanc de Blancs 2018 Dorset, England
12% alcohol. This 25 acre (10 hectare) vineyard was planted on Kimmeridgian chalk soils on the farm of Steven and Bella

Spurrier, and first vintage was 2011. This is bright and fruit focused with taut lemony fruit as well as some richer yellow plum and peach notes, all hemmed in by good acidity and with a touch of sweetness on the finish from the dosage. Great purity and finesse here with good balance, and just a slight dairy hint in the background. 90/100

Oxney Organic Brut 2019 England
11.5% alcohol. Blend of the three classic Champagne varieties. Taut, fresh and lemony with a hint of grilled pineapple as well as a nice chalky edge. An appealing, brisk fizz with a taut, stony, mineral finish. 90/100

Digby Fine English Brut NV England
12% alcohol. From chalky soils in Dorset, Kent, Sussex and Hampshire, this is a blend of the three classic varieties, with a slight emphasis on Pinot Noir. Full malolactic. Base wine has 5% barrel fermentation, 20% reserve wines. Disgorged February 2020. This is toasty and has some nice bready richness, but also some lemony freshness with a taut herbal flourish on the finish, as well as citrus pith and good acidity. There's plenty of generosity, with a touch of peach and pear richness alongside the toastiness. Complex and mouthfilling, showing a touch of development to complement the fruit purity that's really nice. 90/100

Flint Vineyard Charmat Rosé 2021 England
12% alcohol. A vivid pink in colour, this is fresh, joyful and fun with tart cherries and raspberry fruit, with just a hint of sappy greenness and nice acidity. It offers immediate pleasure, but there's a touch of seriousness and true vinosity, too. Lovely stuff. 90/100

Bride Valley Cremant NV Dorset, England
12% alcohol. 59% Chardonnay, 27% Pinot Meunier, 14% Pinot Noir. Residual sugar 10.6 g/l. Lively with nice precision showing pure citrus fruit and a nice acid line. Notes of green apple and lime. 90/100

Nutbourne Vineyards Nutty Vintage 2018 England
12% alcohol. 70% Pinot Noir, 15% Pinot Blanc, 15% Chardonnay. Rs 6 g/l. Bright, linear and fruit drive with appealing citrus fruit. Pretty and expressive with some cherry and plum notes. Focused and very fruity. 89/100

Ashling Park Cuvée NV England
12% alcohol. A blend of 60% Pinot Noir, 30% Chardonnay and 10% Pinot Meunier. Rs 8.1 g/l. Powerful, lively and toasty with broad flavours, including citrus, green apple and peach. 89/100

Ashling Park Sparkling Rosé NV England
12% alcohol. A blend of 80% Pinot Noir and 20% Pinot Meunier. Rs is 4.8 g/l. Orange/yellow in colour. Powerful, spicy and lime with some orange peel and almond. Lots of flavour here. 89/100

Castle Brook Vineyard Blanc de Blancs 2015 England
12% alcohol. 100% Chardonnay, rs 7.7 g/l. Powerful and vivid. Intense. Nice brightness with lovely vivid citrus fruit as well as some toasty notes. Creamy undercurrents. 89/100

High Clandon Estate The Gloriana Cuvée Prestige 2018 England
12% alcohol. 57% Chardonnay, 27% Pinot Noir, 17% Pinot Meunier. Rs 9 g/l. Lively, linear and bright with nice pure lemony fruit and a subtle toastiness. There's a slight sweetness on the finish. 89/100

Woodchester Valley Reserve Cuvée NV England
12% alcohol. Base wine 2019 (71%) with 29% 2018 as a reserve wine. 54% Pinot Noir, 38% Chardonnay, 8% Pinot Meunier. Fresh and fruity with subtle pear skin and toast,

as well as a touch of apple. Lovely purity and fruit here.
89/100

88

Plumpton Centre of Excellence Brut Rosé NV England
Full pink/orange colour. Appealing aromas and flavours of
wild strawberry, ripe apple and green herbs, with a juicy
quality and lots of fruitiness. Nice balance here with an easy
personality. 88/100

**Birchden Vineyards The Charmed Finch Sparkling
Rosé 2020 Sussex, England**
11% alcohol. 100% Pinot Noir, 33 months on lees. Very pale
pink in colour, this is a delicate, slightly sappy traditional
method fizz. Notes of cherry, mandarin and lemon, as well
as a touch of aniseed, with moderate acidity and a soft
texture on the mid-palate. This is pure and well balanced,
and has a light, delicate character. 88/100

Castle Brook Vineyards Classic Cuvée 2017 England
12% alcohol. 43% Chardonnay, 35% Pinot Noir, 22% Pinot
Meunier. Rs 8.6 g/l. Lively, bright and intense with nice
pure fruit and some subtle toasty notes. Good concentration
with a nice acid line. 88/100

87

Silver Reign Charmat of England NV Kent, England
12.5% alcohol. Stylishly packaged, this is a Charmat method
English fizz. It's fruity and appealing on the nose with
melon, white peach and pear notes. The palate is broad, rich,
grapey and fruity with lots of ripe fruit – more than you
normally find in English sparkling, and a hint of pithiness,
with moderate acidity. Rich, fruity and appealing, this is a

real crowd pleaser with a touch of sweetness on the finish. Has a little bite at the end. 87/100

86

Sliverhand Traditional Method Classic Brut NV Kent, England
12% alcohol. The strapline on the back of the bottle is 'defining the new rules of sparkling wine from England.' Tart, fruity and bright with hints of elderflower and honeysuckle, as well as mandarin and citrus on the nose. The palate is fruity and grapey and really accessible with sweet fruit and moderate acidity, as well as a sense of lightness. This is all about pure fruit, with lemon, mandarin and table grape in the mix. Not a typical traditional-method sparkling, it's a real crowd pleaser for those who find most English fizz a bit acidic and challenging. My partner says, 'it's like they forgot something. It's like they didn't add salt in the cooking.' 86/100

Bride Valley Rosé Bella 2018 Dorset, England
12.5% alcohol. 60% Pinot Noir, 30% Chardonnay, 10% Pinot Meunier. Herby and stony with a green edge to the fruit. Tight and compressed. 86/100

85

Silverhand Blanc de Blancs 2018 England
12.5% alcohol. Fruity, exotic and lively with pear and melon notes. Very fruit driven with moderate acidity. It's all about sweet primary fruit. Grapey and a bit confected. It's accessible and easy, but falls flat. 85/100

Pinot Noir, almost ready to pick, September 2023

Vines at Domaine Hugo in early summer

South Downs chalk soils, with some flint

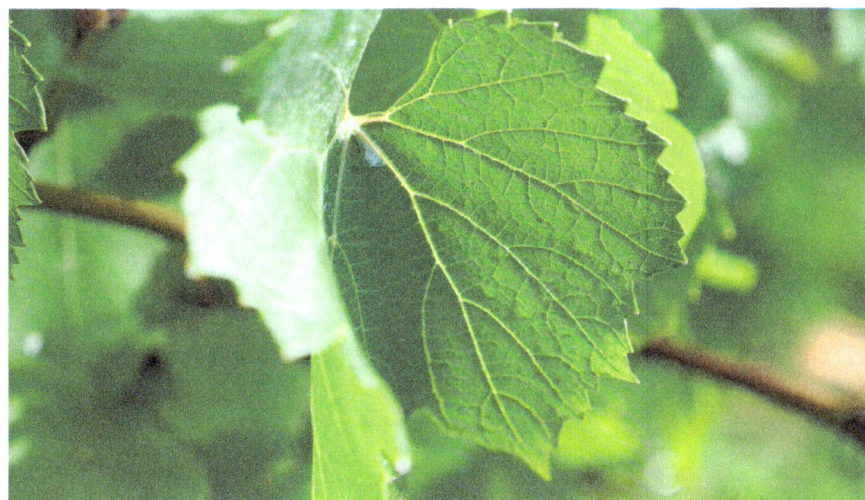

Printed in Great Britain
by Amazon

57020152R00046